A LIFEGUIDE

MW00963108

PSALMS II

Heart Cries to God

12 Studies
for individuals or groups

Juanita Ryan

With Notes for Leaders

INTERVARSITY PRESS
DOWNERS GROVE, ILLINOIS 60515

©1995 by Juanita Ryan

All rights reserved. No part of this book may be reproduced in any form without written permission from InterVarsity Press, P.O. Box 1400, Downers Grove, IL 60515.

InterVarsity Press® is the book-publishing division of InterVarsity Christian Fellowship®, a student movement active on campus at hundreds of universities, colleges and schools of nursing in the United States of America, and a member movement of the International Fellowship of Evangelical Students. For information about local and regional activities, write Public Relations Dept., InterVarsity Christian Fellowship, 6400 Schroeder Rd., P.O. Box 7895, Madison, WI 53707-7895.

LifeGuide® is a registered trademark of InterVarsity Christian Fellowship.

All Scripture quotations, unless otherwise indicated, are taken from the HOLY BIBLE, NEW INTERNATIONAL VERSION®. NIV®. Copyright ©1973, 1978, 1984 by International Bible Society. Used by permission of Zondervan Publishing House. All rights reserved.

Cover photograph: Dennis Frates

ISBN 0-8308-1038-2

Printed in the United States of America ♾

| 20 | 19 | 18 | 17 | 16 | 15 | 14 | 13 | 12 | 11 | 10 | 9 | 8 | 7 | 6 | 5 | 4 | 3 |

| 11 | 10 | 09 | 08 | 07 | 06 | 05 | 04 | 03 | 02 | 01 | 00 |

Contents

Getting the Most
from LifeGuide® Bible Studies

Many of us long to fill our minds and our lives with Scripture. We desire to be transformed by its message. LifeGuide® Bible Studies are designed to be an exciting and challenging way to do just that. They help us to be guided by God's Word in every area of life.

How They Work

LifeGuides have a number of distinctive features. Perhaps the most important is that they are *inductive* rather than *deductive*. In other words, they lead us to *discover* what the Bible says rather than simply *telling* us what it says.

They are also thought-provoking. They help us to think about the meaning of the passage so that we can truly understand what the author is saying. The questions require more than one-word answers.

The studies are personal. Questions expose us to the promises, assurances, exhortations and challenges of God's Word. They are designed to allow the Scriptures to renew our minds so that we can be transformed by the Spirit of God. This is the ultimate goal of all Bible study.

The studies are versatile. They are designed for student, neighborhood and church groups. They are also effective for individual study.

How They're Put Together

LifeGuides also have a distinctive format. Each study need take no more than forty-five minutes in a group setting or thirty minutes in personal study—unless you choose to take more time.

The studies can be used within a quarter system in a church and fit well in a semester or trimester system on a college campus. If a guide has more than thirteen studies, it is divided into two or occasionally three parts of approximately twelve studies each.

LifeGuides use a workbook format. Space is provided for writing answers to each question. This is ideal for personal study and allows group members to prepare in advance for the discussion.

The studies also contain leader's notes. They show how to lead a group discussion, provide additional background information on certain questions, give helpful tips on group dynamics and suggest ways to deal with problems which may arise during the discussion. With such helps, someone with little or no experience can lead an effective study.

Suggestions for Individual Study

1. As you begin each study, pray that God will help you to understand and apply the passage to your life.

2. Read and reread the assigned Bible passage to familiarize yourself with what the author is saying. In the case of book studies, you may want to read through the entire book prior to the first study. This will give you a helpful overview of its contents.

3. A good modern translation of the Bible, rather than the King James Version or a paraphrase, will give you the most help. The New International Version, the New American Standard Bible and the Revised Standard Version are all recommended. However, the questions in this guide are based on the New International Version.

4. Write your answers in the space provided in the study guide. This will help you to express your understanding of the passage clearly.

5. It might be good to have a Bible dictionary handy. Use it to look up any unfamiliar words, names or places.

Suggestions for Group Study

1. Come to the study prepared. Follow the suggestions for individual study mentioned above. You will find that careful preparation will greatly enrich your time spent in group discussion.

2. Be willing to participate in the discussion. The leader of your group will not be lecturing. Instead, he or she will be encouraging the members of the group to discuss what they have learned from the passage. The leader will be asking the questions that are found in this guide. Plan to share what God has taught you in your individual study.

3. Stick to the passage being studied. Your answers should be based on the verses which are the focus of the discussion and not on outside authorities such as commentaries or speakers. This guide deliberately avoids jumping from book to book or passage to passage. Each study focuses on only one

passage. Book studies are generally designed to lead you through the book in the order in which it was written. This will help you follow the author's argument.

4. Be sensitive to the other members of the group. Listen attentively when they share what they have learned. You may be surprised by their insights! Link what you say to the comments of others so the group stays on the topic. Also, be affirming whenever you can. This will encourage some of the more hesitant members of the group to participate.

5. Be careful not to dominate the discussion. We are sometimes so eager to share what we have learned that we leave too little opportunity for others to respond. By all means participate! But allow others to also.

6. Expect God to teach you through the passage being discussed and through the other members of the group. Pray that you will have an enjoyable and profitable time together.

7. If you are the discussion leader, you will find additional suggestions and helpful ideas for each study in the leader's notes. These are found at the back of the guide.

Introducing Psalms II

The psalms are acts of relating to God. In the intense language of poetry, they address God with frankness and urgency. They give voice to our inner turmoil. They teach us to talk to God about life's deepest needs and longings with childlike vulnerability and spontaneity. They immerse us in a spiritual life that is a passionate struggle to love and to know we are loved by God.

The psalms offer us the gifts of expression, courage and celebration—and the gift of raw honesty. The psalms do not attempt to be "nice" or "polite" or even "theologically correct." Instead, they give us permission to talk to God without holding back and to be exactly where we are and who we are with God.

The psalms also offer us the gift of expression. They give us powerful, passionate words and images which express our heart cry to God. The private realties which we hesitate to speak out loud to ourselves or to God are given voice. Our fears, our hopes, our joy, our anger, our longing, our gratitude, our doubt, our worship find full expression here.

In addition, the psalms give us the gift of courage, particularly the courage to acknowledge our vulnerable dependence on God. We greatly prefer to think of ourselves as invulnerable and independent. It takes courage to admit the truth of our dependency on God. But, like all truth, this truth frees us. It frees us to be who we are. It frees us to let God be God, and to let ourselves be his children.

Finally, the psalms give us the gift of celebration. They call us to shout, sing, dance our gratitude and praise to God. The psalms draw us into active worship. They take us by the hand and lead us to a grand party where the gifts of life and love are celebrated and God is praised. As we enter the world of the psalms, we come into God's presence as the vulnerable, honest, needy, spontaneous, joyful children he made us to be.

May you find the gifts of honesty, expression, courage and celebration the psalms offer you. May they bring new depth and vitality to your relationship with God.

Note from the publisher: You may wonder why this guide is titled *Psalms II*. This is the second collection of studies on psalms in the LifeGuide® Bible Study series. The first is entitled *Psalms: Prayers of the Heart* and is by Eugene Peterson. Both of these guides contain studies selected from the entire book of Psalms, rather than focusing on a particular section.

1
A Prayer of Dependence
Psalm 86

Our relationship with God is that of children to a parent, sheep to a shepherd, creatures to the Creator. We are dependent on him for life, for breath, for sustenance, for help in trouble, for love, for forgiveness, for mercy. We may like to think of ourselves as independent and self-sufficient, but we are not. We need God. It is vital that we acknowledge our need because it is the beginning point of our relationship with him. This psalm helps us give voice to our dependence on God.

1. Think of a time when you needed to rely on someone for emotional or physical support. What feelings did you have about depending on that person for help?

2. Read Psalm 86. What is the overall sense you get about the nature of the psalmist's relationship with God?

3. List the many requests the psalmist makes of God.

4. The psalmist describes himself in the first verse as "poor and needy." What is he saying about himself?

5. What reactions would you have to describing yourself as poor and needy?

6. Why does the psalmist need God's help?

7. The psalmist sees God as loving, powerful and actively involved in caring for him. What are some of the specific statements he makes about God?

8. What impact would this view of God have on a person's ability to depend on God?

9. How does the psalmist show his dependence on God throughout this psalm?

_____

10. When is it difficult for you to depend on God?

_____

11. How might the psalmist's dependency on God encourage you to depend more fully on God?

_____

12. In what areas of your life do you need to acknowledge your dependence on God?

2
A Prayer of Longing for God

Psalm 63

Sometimes we feel separated from God. During these times, we may feel much like small children feel when they are separated from their parents— frightened, angry. And we may experience an intense longing for our Parent to return.

Many things can create this sense of separation from God. It might come as a result of a loss or crisis in our lives which leaves us feeling forgotten or uncared for by God. It might come during a time of personal sin or failure when we struggle with fear that God might condemn or reject us. It might come, as it did for this psalmist, as a result of being removed from our community of faith. Whatever the reason, a sense of separation from God can generate life's deepest pain, that of an intense longing for God. This psalm helps us express our longing for God in times when we feel separated from him.

1. Think of a time when you felt especially close to God. What was the experience like for you?

---

2. Read Psalm 63. According to this psalm, David did not experience a constant sense of closeness to God. How does his present experience of God differ from his past experience (vv. 1-2)?

---

3. The psalmist describes his experience of longing for God in verse 1 with the strong physical metaphor of being thirsty in a desert with no sign of water. How is this image an appropriate description of what it feels like to be separated from God?

---

4. In verses 2 and 3 the psalmist describes how in the past he experienced God's presence. What did he experience of God?

---

5. Verse 1 describes a soul which is thirsty, with no chance of finding water. In stark contrast, verse 5 describes a soul which is satisfied with the richest of foods. These pictures contrast the experience of being separated from God and the experience of being close to God. What words or images would you use to describe times when you have felt separated from God?

What words or images would you use to describe times when you felt close to God?

---

6. Because of his longing for connection with God, the psalmist says he will seek God, he will remember God and he will cling to God. The first action he takes is to earnestly seek God (v. 1). What does it mean to seek God?

---

7. The second action he takes is "remembering." Where, when, how and in what way does the psalmist say he "remembers" God (vv. 6-7)?

---

8. What value is there in remembering past experiences of God when we feel separated from him?

---

9. The third action he describes is "clinging." In verse 8 he describes how he clings to God and how God holds him. What is your response to the image of clinging to God?

to the image of being held by God?

---

10. In the final phrases the psalmist responds in joy to the hope of once again experiencing God's presence. How has a sense of God's presence led to joy in your experience?

11. As you think about the actions of seeking, remembering and clinging to God, which of these most closely describes what would be most helpful to you at this time? Explain.

12. Based on this study, make a list of specific actions you can take when you are feeling separated from God.

3
A Prayer of Trust
Psalm 62

Humans come into the world as vulnerable creatures, completely dependent on their parents for their survival. For people to develop a healthy capacity to trust, they need to experience an emotional attachment to a nurturing parent. If children are not greeted with nurturing, empathic responses to their physical, emotional and social needs, or if the relationship with the parent is disrupted, the attachment will be threatened and the capacity to trust will be damaged. Later in life it may be more difficult for them to trust God.

The good news is that God can heal our wounds. He can rebuild our capacity to trust.

Trust is based on a person's character and truthfulness. It is an act of committing oneself to another's good intentions and care. This psalm invites us to risk trusting. It calls us to commit ourselves to God's care.

---

1. What makes a person trustworthy?

2. Read Psalm 62. How does the writer contrast God and humanity?

3. The psalmist talks about resting in God. What pictures come to your mind with these words?

4. How is resting in God a picture of trust?

5. In verse 8 the psalmist draws a parallel between trusting in God and pouring out one's heart to God. How are these related?

6. Verse 10 warns against trusting in material wealth. Why is this such a strong temptation?

7. Where else might you be tempted to place your trust, other than in God?

8. The last two verses depict God as strong and as loving. What images of a strong and loving God are presented in the psalm?

9. What images might you use?

___

10. How does seeing God as strong help you to trust him?

___

11. How does seeing God as loving help you to trust him?

___

12. Write a psalm (or personal prayer) expressing your current feelings about trusting God. Include any fears, hesitations, longings, hope or gratitude you may have.

4
A Prayer of Distress

Psalm 57

Our need for God's presence and care in our lives is a daily reality. We do not always experience this reality, however. As C. S. Lewis wrote in *A Grief Observed,* sometimes "life is so good," we may be "tempted to forget our need of him."* But there are times in our lives when we are acutely aware of our need of God. In times of distress, when we are threatened with loss or harm or even with death, we remember our need of God and we turn to him with great urgency.

Some people feel that they cannot bring their troubles to God. I have often heard people say, "I can't turn to God when I am in distress if I haven't been talking with him all along." And I have heard other people say, "I can't bother God with this, there are many people hurting more than I am." But God invites us to turn to him when we are in distress. Repeatedly in Scripture God says to us, "Call on me in the day of trouble and I will answer you." This is exactly what this psalm helps us to do.

---

1. In times of distress do you generally seek out other people or do you withdraw? Explain what you do and discuss why you might choose these particular behaviors.

2. Read Psalm 57. The title and the introduction to this psalm suggest that it was written by David when he fled into a cave to hide from King Saul, who wanted to kill him. Describe the picture of God's comfort David paints in verse 1.

---

3. In his time of distress David cries out to God (v. 2). What does it mean to "cry out" to God?

---

4. What metaphors does David use in verse 4 to describe the danger he finds himself in?

What feelings do these images evoke?

---

5. How does God intervene for David in his time of distress (vv. 2-3, 6)?

---

6. David responds to God's care in verse 7 by saying that his heart is steadfast. What is the significance of this response?

---

7. David also responds with praise to God. Paraphrase the words of praise David offers to God (vv. 5, 9-11).

8. First Samuel 24 tells the story behind this psalm. Read 24:1-7 and 16-20. How did God take care of David in this time of great distress?

9. Hopefully, most of our times of distress will not be as dramatic as this story from David's life. However, any time of distress is a time when our awareness of our need of God may be heightened. Think of a time when you were in distress. Were you able to cry out to God for help at that time? Why or why not?

10. What was your experience of God like during that time?

11. How might this psalm encourage you in times of distress?

*C. S. Lewis, *A Grief Observed* (New York: Bantam, 1976).

5
A Prayer of Anger

Psalm 94

Mike and John had something in common—they had both been ripped off by their business partners, and they were both angry. Very angry. As they shared their experiences with each other, they discovered an important difference, however. Mike was baffled by what to do with his strong feelings. His anger frightened him and did not seem very spiritual, so most of the time he kept quiet about his sense of outrage at the unfairness of it all. John, on the other hand, had grown up in a church that prayed the psalms. Together they had spoken the psalmist's words of anger and outrage to God. As a result, John was able to talk to God about his anger. He knew he had been grievously wronged and that he was deeply angry. And he knew he could take his anger to God. This psalm is one of the psalms that can help us speak freely to God about our anger.

1. Describe one or two events which left you feeling angry.

How did you handle your anger?

2. Read Psalm 94. The psalmist expresses his anger in a variety of ways. What approaches does he take?

_____

3. For many people admitting anger to God or to anyone seems difficult or unacceptable. This psalm models honesty with ourselves and with God. How difficult is it for you to admit your angry feelings to yourself and to God? Explain.

_____

4. The psalmist addresses God as the Judge and as the one who avenges. What is the meaning of this for the psalmist?

_____

5. In pleading his case before God, what does the psalmist say the wicked have done (vv. 4-7)?

_____

6. In verses 8-10 the psalmist asks several rhetorical questions of God. What statement is he making in these questions?

_____

7. What hope does the psalmist express in verses 12-15?

_____

8. Verse 16 captures the question the psalmist is wrestling with. What words would you use to express this question?

What underlying feelings does this question express?

9. In verses 17-19 the psalmist expresses himself in vulnerable terms. How does he describe the experience of danger and fear that generated his anger?

10. What does he say God did for him in this situation (v. 22)?

11. The psalmist concludes with statements that God will be the Judge (v. 23). Why is this important to remember when we are feeling powerless and outraged in the face of injustice?

12. This psalm shows several constructive ways we can behave when we are angry. It models honesty with ourselves and with God, stating our case to God, acknowledging our vulnerability, trusting God's care and letting God take care of justice. How might this example help you in times of anger?

Which of these behaviors might be especially important for you to follow when you are angry? Explain.

6
A Prayer of Desperation
Psalm 142

I t's cancer." The words shattered the tension in the room. I had been waiting with my friend to find out the results of her biopsy. My friend was calm. She was probably too stunned to feel. I, however, felt desperate. I wanted to scream "No!" I felt frightened, powerless, outraged.

Desperation is an experience of extreme need and helplessness. We feel desperate when life's circumstances overpower us. We feel desperate when our well-being is threatened and we are unable to affect the outcome. This psalm gives voice to our experiences of desperation.

---

1. What kinds of events might cause people to feel desperate?

---

2. Psalm 142 was written by David when he was in a cave, perhaps when he was hiding from Saul (as in study 4). Review 1 Samuel 24:1-2. What about David's situation was desperate?

3. Read Psalm 142. How would you describe David's emotional state?

4. What phrases and images does David use to describe the situation he faces (vv. 3, 6 and 7)?

5. What phrases or images would you use to describe desperate situations you or a loved one have faced?

6. What contrast do you see between David's experiences with people and his experience with God?

7. How would you compare his view of his personal power with his view of God's power?

What is the significance of this contrast when we feel desperate?

8. What would help you to pray with this kind of directness and urgency in times of personal need?

9. What specifically does David ask of God (vv. 6 and 7)?

10. Make a brief list of things you can do when you feel desperate.

11. Write a psalm of your own, allowing yourself to cry out to God on your own behalf, or on behalf of someone else who is facing a desperate situation.

7
A Prayer of Gratitude
Psalm 65

Because I have difficulty receiving gifts or compliments from others, I have had to remind myself to look people in the eyes when they offer me a gift or a compliment and say thank you.

When we are unable to receive the good things that others offer us, we cheat ourselves, and we cheat them. When we are able to say thank you for gifts given, we are able to take the gift in, enjoy it and engage in a personal, intimate way with the giver of the gift.

In the same way, when we express gratitude to God for the gifts he gives us, we enter into a cycle of joyful relating with him. We take in his love, feel a deeper connection with him and experience joy. This psalm invites us to express gratitude to God for his good gifts.

1. What is it like for you to receive a gift or a compliment?

What is it like for you to offer a gift or compliment to someone else?

2. Read Psalm 65. The psalmist expresses gratitude to God for a variety of good gifts. List four categories of gifts this psalm expresses gratitude for.

_____

3. God's great power is acknowledged in this psalm. How is God's power a gift to us?

_____

4. In verse 5 God is called "our Savior, the hope of all the ends of the earth and of the farthest seas." In what ways is God the hope of all the earth and seas?

_____

5. In what ways is God the source of your hope?

_____

6. The psalmist mentions several of God's awesome deeds in verses 6 and 7. What other awesome deeds might you add to the list?

_____

7. Verse 8 offers a picture of the fears and joys common to all people of the earth. How do God's wonders cause us to experience fear?

How do God's wonders call forth songs of joy?

8. Verses 9-13 describe the specific ways in which God tenderly loves and cares for the earth. What thoughts and feelings does this description evoke?

9. What implications does God's care for the earth have for the ways in which we treat the earth?

10. What personal value does expressing gratitude to God have for you?

11. What are you grateful for today?

12. Write a psalm of gratitude or a thank-you letter to God expressing your feelings.

8
A Prayer of Grief
Psalm 102

And grief still feels like fear. Perhaps, more strictly, like suspense. Or like waiting; just hanging around waiting for something to happen. It gives life a permanently provisional feeling. . . . The act of living is different all through. Her absence is like the sky, spread over everything."*

Grief is an experience of deep sorrow over a significant loss. Whether the loss we have suffered is the loss of a loved one, a job, our health or our home, the physical, emotional and spiritual suffering is intense. Grieving is an important spiritual and emotional process that allows us to feel the impact of the loss on our life so that we can slowly take in the reality of our loss and make painful, necessary adaptations. As a part of this process, we need to find people to express our feelings to. And we need to express our feelings over our loss to God. This psalm speaks our anguish to God in times of grief.

1. How would you describe the experience of grief?

2. Read Psalm 102. How does this psalm contrast the fleeting nature of human life and God's eternal existence?

What is the psalmist saying with this contrast?

3. In verses 1-2 the psalmist pleads for God to hear him. Why is this need so urgent in times of grief and distress (vv. 1-2)?

4. How does the psalmist describe his current physical and emotional state (vv. 2-11)?

5. What is it about grief that creates this kind of experience?

6. What thoughts and feelings do you have toward the writer as you read the description of his suffering?

7. How do the writer's descriptions of suffering compare with your experiences of grief?

8. Focus on one of the powerful images the writer uses in verses 3-11 to express his suffering. What meaning does the image convey?

9. The psalmist seems to be blaming God and pleading with God at the same time. What does he blame God for (vv. 8, 10, 23)?

What does he plead for (vv. 1-2, 24)?

10. The writer seems to have mixed feelings about God. What positive perspectives does he express about God (vv. 12-22, 25-28)?

11. Mixed feelings about God are common in times of suffering and grief. What about times of grief might create these mixed feelings?

12. What experience have you had with mixed feelings toward God in times of grief?

13. How could this psalm help you in times of grief?

---

*C. S. Lewis, *A Grief Observed* (New York: Bantam, 1976) pp. 39, 13.

9
A Prayer of Despair
Psalm 88

I give up," Nancy said as she buried her face in her hands.

Nancy was not a passive person. She worked hard as a single mother to provide for her children. She had developed a good support system for herself. She was actively, compassionately engaged in life. But a series of losses had left her deeply shaken. Everything she had worked so hard for seemed to be gone. Nancy felt defeated. And without hope.

Despair is hopeless resignation. Or, as the psalmist expresses it, despair is a time when "darkness" becomes our "closest friend."

---

1. What pictures come to mind when you think of a person who is experiencing despair?

---

2. Read Psalm 88. What evidence is there of despair in this psalm?

3. What emotional impact did you experience as you read this psalm?

4. Contrast the first and last verses of this psalm. Most psalms which express strong doubts end with hope or praise. This psalm ends with doubt and despair. What is it like to be left with unresolved questions?

5. Restate in your own words the suffering that the psalmist describes in verses 3-5.

6. At the end of verse 5 the writer is addressing God and describes himself as a person "whom you remember no more . . . cut off from your care." How might a fear that God has forgotten us and does not care about us contribute to feelings of despair?

7. The writer blames God for his desperate situation. What does he say to blame God (vv. 6-9, 15-18)?

8. What reactions do you have to his blaming God?

9. In verses 13 and 14 the psalmist talks about how he continues to pray even though God seems distant and rejecting. What might be causing him to continue to call out to God?

10. What is the value of continuing to talk to God when God seems distant and rejecting?

11. Think of a time when it was difficult for you to talk to God. What was that experience like for you?

12. What would you like to say to God about the areas in life that feel "dark" or hopeless to you?

13. What actions might you take when things seem hopeless?

10
A Prayer When God Is Silent

Psalm 44

Is not God silent about Stalingrad? What do we hear above and under its ruins? Do we not hear the roar of artillery, the tumult of the world and the cries of the dying? But where is the voice of God? When we think of God, is it not suddenly so quiet, so terribly quiet, in the witch's kitchen of this hell, that one can hear a pin drop even though grenades are bursting around us? There is neither voice nor answer."*

We have not all lived through the atrocities of war. But we all are vulnerable to loss and trauma. The silence of God is perhaps one of life's most frightening experiences. What do we do? How do we proceed when God is silent? Do we withdraw in fear? Do we give up all hope? That is certainly our temptation. But this psalm shows us another way. It opens the way for us to pursue God even when he is silent.

---

1. Think of a time when a friend did not respond to letters or phone messages for a long time. What was your reaction to his or her silence?

2. Read Psalm 44. How does the writer contrast God in the past (vv. 1-8) with God in the present (vv. 9-16)?

3. What strikes you as you read the writer's description of God's care?

4. What strikes you as you read the writer's description of God's silence?

5. The psalmist argues with God that the situation he and his people find themselves in is not fair. How does he express this (vv. 17-22)?

6. What is the significance of this plea for fairness and justice?

7. The psalmist summarizes his accusations against God in verses 23 and 24. What does he accuse God of?

8. What would it be like for you to talk to God in this way?

9. In the final phrase of the psalm, the writer appeals to God's unfailing love. This is a dramatic contrast to the accusations he has just made. How can these be reconciled?

10. Think of a time when it seemed God was silent. How did your experience at that time compare with the experiences described in this psalm?

11. Think of a time when you experienced God's unfailing love. How would you describe that experience?

12. What encouragement does this psalm offer you for times when God seems silent?

13. What might help you hang onto your faith when God seems silent?

---

*Helmut Thielicke, *The Silence of God* (Grand Rapids, Mich.: Eerdmans, 1962).

11
A Prayer for Hope
Psalm 130

During a time of difficult waiting I expressed the contrast between waiting with hope and waiting without hope:

> When waiting is expectant,
> I move through the light and shadows
> of life's in-between times content.
> Able to see the apricot tree laced with white explosions
> while it is yet dead wood.
> Able to hear in the silence the music of your voice,
> greeting me with grace.
>
> But when waiting is threatened,
> I bear in raging anguish the nightmare possibility
> of no return of spring or you.
> Waiting stretches me across a torture rack of longing.
> Afraid to hope or want or breathe again.
> Blind, deaf, cold with fright
> I wait.

Hope is necessary. It gives us the strength to keep going through the tough times. It gives life joy and meaning in the good times. However, when hope has been repeatedly disappointed, it slips away. This psalm offers a picture of this struggle. The writer is without much hope. Yet, he puts himself in a place of allowing for the possibility of hope. As we pray with him, we too can begin to wait with growing expectation. We too can nurture our hope.

1. How would you describe the experience of hope?

How would you describe the experience of hopelessness?

2. Read Psalm 130. The psalm begins with a cry to the Lord from "out of the depths" (v. 1). What pictures come to mind as you read this phrase?

What emotions is the writer expressing in this phrase?

3. The psalmist's distress seems to be related to a struggle with guilt. How can guilt lead to hopelessness?

4. Verses 3 and 4 tell us that God forgives. How does the promise of forgiveness contribute to hope?

5. Verse 5 says, "I wait . . . my soul waits." What is the relationship between waiting and hope?

6. The psalmist then uses the metaphor of watchmen (v. 6) to describe the experience of hope. What does he convey with this image?

---

7. The psalmist struggles between hopelessness and hope. Why is it sometimes a struggle to hope?

---

8. What area of life is difficult for you to be hopeful about?

---

9. What reasons does the psalmist give for hoping in the Lord (vv. 7-8)?

---

10. What reasons do you have for hoping in the Lord?

---

11. How have you grown spiritually as you have struggled to wait with hope for the Lord?

---

12. How might this psalm help you to hope in the Lord?

12
A Prayer of Joy
Psalm 66

Life was not intended by God to be a joyless ordeal. As much as it might surprise some of us, it is actually God's desire for us to experience joy. Joy is an act of relating to God with vulnerable, unselfconscious gratitude for the good gifts he gives. Joy comes when we experience and acknowledge God's love and care for us, when we allow ourselves to express our gratitude for his love with emotional and physical energy. Joy is the celebration of God's love. This psalm invites us to experience joy.

1. Think of a time when you experienced joy. What evoked this feeling in you?

How would you describe it?

2. Read Psalm 66. The writer calls us to action (vv. 1, 2, 3, 5, 8 and 16). What does he call us to do?

3. How are each of these behaviors related to the experience or the expression of joy?

4. What does the section in the middle of this psalm (vv. 8-12) tell us about the cause for this particular expression of joy?

5. How might this kind of experience lead to joy?

6. Verses 13-15 talk about offering animal sacrifices as an expression of joy and worship. A person's livestock was the equivalent of our personal bank accounts. How can giving materially be an expression of gratitude and joy?

7. Verses 16-20 are a more personal account of what the Lord has done. What does the writer say the Lord has done for him?

8. How might this kind of experience lead to joy?

_____

9. In addition to the actions listed in question 2, what ways of expressing joy to God are described in this psalm?

What other ways of expressing joy to God would you add?

_____

10. In what ways are joy, praise and worship related?

_____

11. It is important to realize that this psalm is not about pretending to be joyful when it is more honest or appropriate to be grieving or angry. What dangers are there in pretending to be joyful when we are not?

_____

12. Why is it important to allow ourselves to experience and express joy?

_____

13. What joy would you like to express to God?

Leader's Notes

Leading a Bible discussion can be an enjoyable and rewarding experience. But it can also be *scary*—especially if you've never done it before. If this is your feeling, you're in good company. When God asked Moses to lead the Israelites out of Egypt, he replied, "O Lord, please send someone else to do it!" (Ex 4:13).

When Solomon became king of Israel, he felt the task was beyond his abilities. "I am only a little child and do not know how to carry out my duties. . . . Who is able to govern this great people of yours?" (1 Kings 3:7, 9).

When God called Jeremiah to be a prophet, he replied, "Ah, Sovereign LORD, . . . I do not know how to speak; I am only a child" (Jer 1:6).

The list goes on. The apostles were "unschooled, ordinary men" (Acts 4:13). Timothy was young, frail and frightened. Paul's "thorn in the flesh" made him feel weak. But God's response to all of his servants—including you—is essentially the same: "My grace is sufficient for you" (2 Cor 12:9). Relax. God helped these people in spite of their weaknesses, and he can help you in spite of your feelings of inadequacy.

There is another reason why you should feel encouraged. Leading a Bible discussion is not difficult if you follow certain guidelines. You don't need to be an expert on the Bible or a trained teacher. The suggestions listed below should enable you to effectively and enjoyably fulfill your role as leader.

Preparing to Lead

1. Ask God to help you understand and apply the passage to your own life. Unless this happens, you will not be prepared to lead others. Pray too for the various members of the group. Ask God to give you an enjoyable and profitable time together studying his Word.

2. As you begin each study, read and reread the assigned Bible passage to familiarize yourself with what the author is saying. In the case of book studies, you may want to read through the entire book prior to the first study. This will give you a helpful overview of its contents.

3. This study guide is based on the New International Version of the Bible. It will help you and the group if you use this translation as the basis for your study and discussion. Encourage others to use the NIV also, but allow them the freedom to use whatever translation they prefer.

4. Carefully work through each question in the study. Spend time in meditation and reflection as you formulate your answers.

5. Write your answers in the space provided in the study guide. This will help you to express your understanding of the passage clearly.

6. It might help you to have a Bible dictionary handy. Use it to look up any unfamiliar words, names or places. (For additional help on how to study a passage, see chapter five of *Leading Bible Discussions,* IVP.)

7. Once you have finished your own study of the passage, familiarize yourself with the leader's notes for the study you are leading. These are designed to help you in several ways. First, they tell you the purpose the study guide author had in mind while writing the study. Take time to think through how the study questions work together to accomplish that purpose. Second, the notes provide you with additional background information or comments on some of the questions. This information can be useful if people have difficulty understanding or answering a question. Third, the leader's notes can alert you to potential problems you may encounter during the study.

8. If you wish to remind yourself of anything mentioned in the leader's notes, make a note to yourself below that question in the study.

Leading the Study

1. Begin the study on time. Unless you are leading an evangelistic Bible study, open with prayer, asking God to help you to understand and apply the passage.

2. Be sure that everyone in your group has a study guide. Encourage them to prepare beforehand for each discussion by working through the questions in the guide.

3. At the beginning of your first time together, explain that these studies are meant to be discussions not lectures. Encourage the members of the group to participate. However, do not put pressure on those who may be hesitant to speak during the first few sessions.

4. Read the introductory paragraph at the beginning of the discussion. This will orient the group to the passage being studied.

5. Read the passage aloud if you are studying one chapter or less. You may choose to do this yourself, or someone else may read if he or she has been asked to do so prior to the study. Longer passages may occasionally be read in parts at different times during the study. Some studies may cover several chapters. In such cases reading aloud would probably take too much time, so the group members should simply read the assigned passages prior to the study.

6. As you begin to ask the questions in the guide, keep several things in mind. First, the questions are designed to be used just as they are written. If you wish, you may simply read them aloud to the group. Or you may prefer to express them in your own words. However, unnecessary rewording of the questions is not recommended.

Second, the questions are intended to guide the group toward understanding and applying the *main idea* of the passage. The author of the guide has stated his or her view of this central idea in the *purpose* of the study in the leader's notes. You should try to understand how the passage expresses this idea and how the study questions work together to lead the group in that direction.

There may be times when it is appropriate to deviate from the study guide. For example, a question may have already been answered. If so, move on to the next question. Or someone may raise an important question not covered in the guide. Take time to discuss it! The important thing is to use discretion. There may be many routes you can travel to reach the goal of the study. But the easiest route is usually the one the author has suggested.

7. Avoid answering your own questions. If necessary, repeat or rephrase them until they are clearly understood. An eager group quickly becomes passive and silent if they think the leader will do most of the talking.

8. Don't be afraid of silence. People may need time to think about the question before formulating their answers.

9. Don't be content with just one answer. Ask, "What do the rest of you think?" or "Anything else?" until several people have given answers to the question.

10. Acknowledge all contributions. Try to be affirming whenever possible. Never reject an answer. If it is clearly wrong, ask, "Which verse led you to that conclusion?" or again, "What do the rest of you think?"

11. Don't expect every answer to be addressed to you, even though this will probably happen at first. As group members become more at ease, they will begin to truly interact with each other. This is one sign of a healthy discussion.

12. Don't be afraid of controversy. It can be very stimulating. If you don't resolve an issue completely, don't be frustrated. Move on and keep it in mind for later. A subsequent study may solve the problem.

13. Stick to the passage under consideration. It should be the source for answering the questions. Discourage the group from unnecessary cross-referencing. Likewise, stick to the subject and avoid going off on tangents.

14. Periodically summarize what the *group* has said about the passage. This helps to draw together the various ideas mentioned and gives continuity to the study. But don't preach.

15. Conclude your time together with conversational prayer. Be sure to ask God's help to apply those things which you learned in the study.

16. End on time.

Many more suggestions and helps are found in *Leading Bible Discussions* (IVP). Reading and studying through that would be well worth your time.

Components of Small Groups
A healthy small group should do more than study the Bible. There are four components you should consider as you structure your time together.

Nurture. Being a part of a small group should be a nurturing and edifying experience. You should grow in your knowledge and love of God and each other. If we are to properly love God, we must know and keep his commandments (Jn 14:15). That is why Bible study should be a foundational part of your small group. But you can be nurtured by other things as well. You can memorize Scripture, read and discuss a book, or occasionally listen to a tape of a good speaker.

Community. Most people have a need for close friendships. Your small group can be an excellent place to cultivate such relationships. Allow time for informal interaction before and after the study. Have a time of sharing during the meeting. Do fun things together as a group, such as a potluck supper or a picnic. Have someone bring refreshments to the meeting. Be creative!

Worship. A portion of your time together can be spent in worship and prayer. Praise God together for who he is. Thank him for what he has done and is doing in your lives and in the world. Pray for each other's needs. Ask God to help you to apply what you have learned. Sing hymns together.

Mission. Many small groups decide to work together in some form of outreach. This can be a practical way of applying what you have learned. You can host a series of evangelistic discussions for your friends or neighbors. You can visit people at a home for the elderly. Help a widow with cleaning or repair jobs around her home. Such projects can have a transforming influence on your group.

For a detailed discussion of the nature and function of small groups, read *Small Group Leaders' Handbook* or *Good Things Come in Small Groups* (both from IVP).

General Note

The psalms are deeply emotive prayers, written in the intense language of poetry. To engage with the psalms is to engage strong feelings. Members of the group will have different responses to talking together about feelings. Talking and listening to feelings may come easily for some. For others, talking or listening to emotional pain may feel uncomfortable.

Acknowledge both that the psalms are full of strong feelings and that there is bound to be some discomfort in talking together about feelings. The group might want to take time to discuss what they anticipate, expect, fear and need in regard to this issue. Make it clear that people always have a choice about what they share, and that no one is required to share when it is uncomfortable to do so. On the other hand, groups such as this provide the opportunity for stretching and growing, so some risk-taking and "moving out of one's comfort zone" can be a good thing.

The group needs to agree on two commitments. First, whatever is shared in the group will be treated as confidential and will not be shared outside the group without specific permission from the person. And second, they will listen to each other with respect—being cautious about giving advice and solutions, responding to the person who shared with simple statements of gratitude for their sharing.

A very helpful way to interact with the psalms is to write a responsive psalm of one's own, expressing similar feelings or concerns as those expressed in that particular psalm. This is something your group might want to do with each psalm. If so, it is important to know that this is not meant to be a creative-writing exercise, but a free-writing exercise. It is an opportunity to write out a prayer in whatever form it takes. Encourage people not to edit, but to write as spontaneously as they can. Invite those who want to to read their psalms out loud as a prayer.

Study 1. A Prayer of Dependence. Psalm 86.

Purpose: To acknowledge our dependency on God.

Question 2. Note the writer's direct, frank, unselfconscious expression of need. The psalmist evidences a sense of childlike dependence on God's love and goodness.

Question 4. In describing himself as "poor and needy," the psalmist is honestly acknowledging his need and appealing to God for help. He is needy, and since God made him and his needs, he brings himself and his needs to God. George Macdonald offered a perspective on this when he wrote:

It is God to whom every hunger, every aspiration, every desire, every longing of our nature is to be referred. He made them all—made us the creatures of a thousand necessities—and have we no claim on him? . . . The child has and must have, a claim on the Father, a claim which it is the joy of the Father's heart to acknowledge. A created need is a created claim. God is the origin of both need and supply, the Father of our necessities, the abundant giver of the good things. Gloriously he meets the claims of his child! (*Discovering the Character of God,* compiled by Michael R. Phillips [Minneapolis: Bethany House Publishers, 1989], pp. 206-7.)

Question 5. The reactions of the group to describing themselves as "poor and needy" will, of course, be varied. But it is common for us to be very uncomfortable with such a description. We want to be self-reliant and independent. We are not. It is a myth that protects us from the painful reality that we are vulnerable.

Question 6. The psalmist needs help because "the arrogant are attacking" him, "a band of ruthless men" are seeking his life (v. 14). The psalmist is facing a situation that is too big for him. He is overwhelmed.

It might be useful to point out that most people do not have someone stalking them to kill them. But there will be times when our life or the life of someone close to us may be threatened with illness. There may be times when we feel threatened in other ways (financially, for example) that are overwhelming to us. We all experience many days that would qualify as "days of trouble" (v. 7). We all need God's help in ways similar to what the psalmist experienced. We all have troubles that are too big for us to handle alone.

Question 8. One reason we may have a need to see ourselves as self-sufficient is that many of us experienced shaming for our needs in our most dependent years. Because parents are less than perfect, and sometimes significantly less than what we needed, the experience of being actively cared for by someone who is loving and powerful may feel unfamiliar to us. To begin to see God in this way can help us give up our defense of self-sufficiency and begin to let ourselves depend on God more fully.

Another reason we may see ourselves as self-sufficient is that self-sufficiency is highly valued by our society. We have heroes who teach us to believe we are supposed to "pull ourselves up by our own bootstraps" and fight off all enemies single-handedly.

Question 9. The group may have difficulty identifying evidence of dependence on God. The psalmist describes his dependency on God. He identifies his neediness and contrasts it with God's love and power. He makes many direct requests and appeals that come out of his needs. He clearly knows he cannot take care of himself. He knows he needs God.

Question 11. The psalmist models a level of honest humility and dependency on God that our society tends to scorn. His example can give us permission to acknowledge the reality of our need of God, and his expression can help us find ways of expressing those needs specifically.

Study 2. A Prayer of Longing for God. Psalm 63.

Purpose: To express our longing for God in times when we feel separated from him.

Question 3. This metaphor might be seen in several ways. It is a metaphor of dying. It is a metaphor of intense suffering and longing. And it is a metaphor of a person with a single-minded focus—there is only one thing in all the world that a thirsty person in a desert wants. We need God in the same way that we need water. They are basic to life. When we see no sign of God anywhere, we experience deep suffering and intense longing, and we might fear that we will die.

Question 4. The psalmist felt closest to God when he was in the sanctuary—in the place of worship, with a community of believers. You might want to encourage the group to discuss the role of the community of believers in their experience of closeness to God. Some may have had negative experiences with churches. Some may relate very much to what the psalmist is expressing.

Question 6. Help the group discuss the perspectives and the behaviors involved in seeking God. Perspectives might include a sense of awareness, of being on the lookout for, of being open to, of being motivated to find. Behaviors might include studying Scripture, praying and being with other believers.

Question 9. In Deuteronomy 30:20 we are told to "Love the Lord your God, listen to his voice, and hold fast to him." Clinging—or holding fast—to God brings to mind a young child hanging on for dear life to a loving parent. This might be a comforting image for some. For others it might be difficult. Give the group permission to discuss their honest reactions.

Question 12. These lists can be done individually and then discussed by the group, or the group can make a list together.

Study 3. A Prayer of Trust. Psalm 62.

Purpose: To learn to rest more fully in God's love.

Question 2. God is described as a rock, a refuge, a fortress, a place of rest and safety that is reliable, permanent, constant. God is also described as strong and loving. Humanity, by contrast, is described as opportunistic (they fully intend to topple this tottering wall), as deceitful—"blessing with the mouth while cursing with the heart" and as "only a breath."

Question 4. Resting and trust both have to do with relaxing, letting go of anxiety, leaning into, feeling held and feeling secure enough to let down our guard and be vulnerable.

Question 5. You might help the group talk about what is involved when we pour out our heart to someone. It involves intimate disclosure of our deepest needs and feelings. It is a vulnerable act which is possible only when we have some sense that the other person will not judge us or reject us or mock us. It is based in trust that the other person will listen, care, understand, empathize and respond to us.

Question 8. When the images of *mighty rock, refuge* and *fortress* are understood to be set in the open desert, where the sun was scorching, the wind could be merciless and one could be an easy prey to enemies, these images take on new depth. In these images God is seen as reliable, kind, protective, concerned. He is always there to run to, to hold us and protect us, to comfort and care for us. He is strong. He is loving. More specifically, he is strong and loving on our behalf.

Question 9. Encourage the group to put some effort into coming up with images of God as strong and loving. The images used in the psalms came out of common material realties of the day; we do not see fortresses on our way to work. Images are powerful when they are connected to our everyday experiences. Encourage the group to discuss the significance of the images they do come up with. You might ask: "What does the image mean to you?" or "What would it be like to see God in this way?"

Question 12. Information on writing a responsive psalm is at the beginning of this section under "general note."

Study 4. A Prayer of Distress. Psalm 57.

Purpose: To learn to call on God in times of distress.

Question 2. Encourage the group to reflect on the image of taking refuge in the shadow of God's wings. This can be seen as a chick hiding under his mother's wing. It is a picture of being incredibly close, of being protected, of being intimately loved. It is also a picture of the hen putting herself between the chick and his aggressor, protecting him with her life.

Question 4. The group might need help to see that "crying out" is an instinctive, heartfelt, urgent, desperate call for help. When we "cry out," there is no time for face-saving measures or for pretense. When we "cry out," we reveal ourselves; we are real. This is how the psalms help us to relate to God.

This is the language of prayer: men and women calling out their trouble—

pain, guilt, doubt, despair—to God. Their lives are threatened. If they don't get help they will be dead, or diminished to some critical degree. The language of prayer is forged in the crucible of trouble. When we can't help ourselves and call for help, when we don't like where we are and want out, when we don't like who we are and want a change, we use primal language, and this language becomes the root language of prayer. . . . We must let the Psalms train us in prayer language—the language of intimacy, of relationship, of "I and Thou," of personal love. (Eugene Peterson, *Answering God* [San Francisco: Harper & Row, 1989], pp. 35 and 40.)

Question 6. To be steadfast is to be deeply committed to another person. Help the group discuss both the difficulty and the value of staying committed to God in times of distress.

Question 8. Saul, who was a madman by this time, took three thousand of his finest fighting men with him to hunt down David and his men. It must have seemed an impossible situation. But God protected David in an unexpected way.

It would be helpful to point out that there is a comic nature to the story of Saul relieving himself in the dark cave where David hid. God took the madman Saul away from his three thousand men and put him in a vulnerable situation with David. This unexpected, creative, surprising twist to the story should not be missed.

Question 9. Encourage the group to discuss the permission that this psalm, and others, gives for relating to God out of our need. The psalms can free us. They can help us get past our shame and fear. They can help us be childlike with God.

Study 5. A Prayer of Anger. Psalm 94.

Purpose: To learn to bring our anger to God.

Question 2. The psalmist takes several steps in expressing his anger. First he calls God in as the Judge to hear his complaint. Then he makes his complaint and stresses the injustice of the situation. He later appeals to God's authority and power. Finally, he cries out for protection and justice.

Question 4. In his *Reflections on the Psalms,* C. S. Lewis discusses the meaning for the psalmist of seeing God as Judge. He writes:

If there is any thought at which a Christian trembles it is the thought of God's "judgment." . . . It was therefore with great surprise that I first noticed how the Psalmists talk about the judgments of God. . . . Judgment is apparently an occasion of universal rejoicing. People ask for it. . . . The reason for this soon becomes very plain. The ancient Jews, like ourselves, think of God's judgment in terms of an earthly court of justice. The difference is that the

Christian pictures the case to be tried as a criminal case with himself in the dock; the Jew pictures it as a civil case with himself as the plaintiff. The one hopes for acquittal, or rather for pardon; the other hopes for a resounding triumph with heavy damages. . . . Behind this lies an age-old and almost world-wide experience which we have been spared. In most places and times it has been very difficult for the "small man" to get his case heard. . . . We need not therefore be surprised if the Psalms, and the Prophets, are full of the longing for judgment, and regard the announcement that "judgment" is coming as good news. (*Reflections on the Psalms* [New York: Harcourt Brace & World, 1958], pp. 9-11.)

Question 5. Lead the group in seeing that the "wicked" that the psalmist is angry with have acted arrogantly, boasted, oppressed and crushed the people, and have murdered defenseless people, including widows, the fatherless and aliens. The psalmist is specific with God about the wrongs that have been done. He makes it clear not only that he is angry, but why he is angry.

Question 6. The questions the psalmist asks could be reduced to three dramatic statements: God hears, God sees, God knows.

Question 7. The hope the psalmist holds onto is that in spite of the way things seem, God has not forsaken them or forgotten them, but will bring justice to this terribly unjust situation.

Question 8. The psalmist's question could be paraphrased simply: "Who will help me?" He is feeling powerless, helpless, overwhelmed, frightened.

Question 11. Help the group to discuss the value of leaving justice to God. When we are angry, we often want to hurt back, to seek revenge. In fact, our lives can become consumed by the need for revenge. But we are not the Judge. God is. We can let go of the drive for revenge that might otherwise destroy us. We can also let go of the bitterness that might eat away at us inside. This does not mean that we should be passive or fail to take appropriate steps to protect ourselves or to seek action against injustice. But it does mean that we can give our anger to God and trust the outcome to him.

Study 6. A Prayer of Desperation. Psalm 142.

Purpose: To give voice to our desperation, learning to call on God for help.

Question 1. If you have a strong level of trust in your group, then you may want to ask, "What events have left you feeling desperate?"

Question 2. Saul was the king. He had three thousand of his finest fighters with him. And Saul was irrationally jealous, bent on doing away with David. The odds were overwhelmingly in Saul's favor. David's life was in great danger.

Question 5. Encourage the group to take some time with finding images. Let them brainstorm, suggesting whatever images come to mind. Examples might include being run over by a truck, living under a black stormcloud, falling into a well. Explore the meaning and the emotional impact of these images.

Question 7. Help the group discuss David's awareness of his powerlessness and his sense of God's power. David saw himself "faint," alone, facing an enemy who was "too strong" for him. He saw God as a refuge, guide and Savior.

Question 8. The group might need guidance in discussing the barriers that prevent them from approaching God with directness and urgency. One of the gifts the psalms offer us is the permission and help we might need to learn this kind of frank approach to God.

Question 10. When we feel desperate we need to remember that we do not have to be alone. We can ask friends for prayer support, for their presence with us. We can call on God for help.

Question 11. Information on writing a responsive psalm is at the beginning of this section under "general note."

Study 7. A Prayer of Gratitude. Psalm 65.

Purpose: To experience the joy of saying "thank you" to God.

Question 2. The psalmist expresses gratitude for forgiveness (v. 3); relationship (vv. 4-5); creation (vv. 6-8); sustaining, loving care (vv. 9-13).

Question 3. God is powerful. This can be either good news or bad news. Help the group to discuss the significance of the fact that God uses his power to help us, not as a weapon to harm us. In this psalm we reflect on how God uses his power to protect, provide, create and save.

Question 4. You might help the group identify God as the "hope of the earth and seas" by leading a brief discussion about the many ways God sustains the earth and all living things. As Creator, he is highly involved in an ongoing way with his creation. More specifically for us as humans, he is our hope as Creator, Sustainer and as Savior.

Question 6. Encourage all kinds of responses from the group. There are many awesome deeds that God does, some global, some very personal.

Question 7. Help the group discuss the meaning of the fear of God that we experience when we see his wonders. It is a fear that is based in the reality that God is all-powerful, that he is the Creator and we are creatures, that he is infinite and we are finite. It is a fear of respect and appropriate humility. The contrasting joy in response to these same wonders is intriguing. We experience joy because we see that God uses his power to provide us with gifts of beauty and life.

Question 9. This text describes God's tender love for all he has made and compels us to share his perspective. God has given us the gift of his creation. One way to express gratitude for a gift is to cherish, value and take good care of it.

Study 8. A Prayer of Grief. Psalm 102.

Purpose: To learn to pray in times of grief.

Question 2. It is important to realize that the psalmist did not have a sense of life after death.

It seems quite clear that in most parts of the Old Testament there is little or no belief in a future life; certainly no belief that is of any religious importance. The word translated "Sheol" in our version of the psalms means simply "the land of the dead," the state of all the dead, good and bad alike, Sheol. (C. S. Lewis, *Reflections on the Psalms* [New York: Harcourt Brace & World], 1958, p. 36)

As a result, the psalmist is saying to God, "It really isn't fair that you should cut me off in midlife, when my life as a human is so short and your life is eternal. It isn't fair, and what good will it do anybody?"

Question 3. Help the group discuss the reality that we can feel separated from God in times of loss or distress, because it can feel as if God has forgotten us or turned away from us when bad things happen. This sense of separation from God adds a spiritual crisis on top of the original crisis of the loss. We very much need to feel God's presence when we are faced with loss, yet we may feel his absence instead. It is out of this struggle that the psalmist speaks with such urgency to God.

Question 4. Grief is a powerful physical, emotional and spiritual experience. Sometimes when we lose someone or something close to us we say we feel as if "we have lost a part of ourselves." We become deeply attached to persons, places, dreams. The loss of any of these requires an enormous adaptation on our part—one that we would rather avoid.

Years ago I spoke to a twenty-year-old woman whose father had died when she was eight. She had never grieved his loss. She had spent the twelve years after his death imagining that he would come back and that life would be like it was before he left. This fantasy had left her out of touch with reality, unable to cope or to form new relationships. But to face the reality of his death was to feel the full impact of the loss. She needed, as we all do, support from others to do the hard work of grieving. This hard work ("grief work") requires that we talk at length about the person or place or object or dream that we have lost, feel the sadness and anger and fear the loss creates, and slowly accept the reality.

Question 5. Give the group permission to share their honest reactions to the writer's suffering. They may feel repulsion or identification; they may feel like they don't want to hear about it, or they may feel empathy. Whatever each person might feel at the time, there is a reason for their reaction. If members seem to feel comfortable, you might ask them what makes them react the way they do.

Question 10. This question is related to the discussion in study 2 on longing for God. Because the experience of loss and grief can leave us feeling separated from God, as if he has left us, we may react with the mixture of feelings that small children have when separated from their parents. We may feel anger, fear and a deep yearning for a reuniting with God.

Question 12. If it feels comfortable and if time allows, you may want to conclude with the following question: "What grief are you aware of (over a loss you have suffered—recent or long past) that you need to express to God?" Use this as a basis for praying for one another.

Study 9. A Prayer of Despair. Psalm 88.

Purpose: To learn to talk with God, even in the midst of despair.

Question 4. Help the group to discuss the extreme discomfort we often feel with unanswered questions and unresolved doubts. Encourage discussion of where this discomfort comes from and what might help in the face of unanswered questions.

Question 6. Our belief in God's personal love and care for us is a primary source of hope and strength. When we are afraid that God has forgotten us and no longer cares about us, then we are left feeling not only unprotected, but even worse, unloved and unwanted. This can lead to despair.

Question 8. People may have a variety of responses to the psalmist's statements to God which hold God responsible for his suffering. Some may hear the anger in these statements. Anger with God is often frightening for us. But, the psalmist relates in an honest, uncensored way to God. Others may sympathize with the feeling that when bad things happen it seems that God must have done them. If he is powerful and loving it is very difficult to understand why he doesn't protect us from hardship. Most people will identify with these feelings the psalmist is experiencing in relation to God. But many people may not feel free to express these struggles to God or to others. This psalm might help group members feel freer to voice their spiritual distress.

Question 9. The psalmist's longing for God, his desperation and despair, and an undying seed of hope that God may not be as rejecting as he fears may all have kept him calling out to God.

Question 10. Our most fundamental human need is a relationship with God. No matter how distant or rejecting we sometimes may fear God to be, we must continue pursuing him because we need him.

This is an important point that really is at the heart of the psalms. It might be useful to spend some time reflecting together on this underlying teaching: no matter what, we need to keep talking to God—not in the form of ritualistic or pious, pretending prayers, but in honest spontaneous prayers.

Study 10. A Prayer When God Is Silent. Psalm 44.

Purpose: To discover that we need to pray, even when God is silent.

Question 3. You might want to focus especially on verse 3, which is highly personal in its expression of the experience of God's love.

Question 4. Discuss the uncomfortable fact that the way the psalmist describes God's silence is that he sees God as cruel, as actively punishing them by his lack of responsiveness. This is not a doctrinal statement asserting that God is cruel. It is a statement from the gut about how it feels when God is not responsive to us, when he does not save or protect us.

Question 9. The group may need help to see that the whole psalm is actually an appeal to God's love. It is because of God's love that God will not want his people to experience his silence as harshness. It is because of his love that he will eventually respond to their need.

Question 13. It is important for the group to realize that when it seems that God is silent, they are not alone with this experience. Many people struggle with this from time to time, including many of God's most faithful. If we are able to talk about our experience with other believers and ask for their support, understanding and prayers, we will not be so alone in these times. Be sure to pray for each other and reach out to any in the group who may be feeling discouraged in some way.

Study 11. A Prayer for Hope. Psalm 130.

Purpose: To nurture hope.

Questions 3-4. The group will undoubtedly see that guilt separates us from God and that forgiveness restores our relationship with him. But the further question here is, "Why is our hope so tied to our relationship with God?" The answer has to do with the nature of hope. Hope is not necessarily believing that everything will be fine. Hope is believing that God will be with us—that no matter what happens, God will be with us, holding onto us.

Question 5. It is important to note that waiting for God and waiting for hope are seen as one and the same, because our hope is in God.

We need to remind ourselves daily that we do not serve the god-of-relent-less-cheerfulness, or the god-of-naiveté, or the god-of-blind-optimism. We serve the God of hope. . . . We can come to him with our fear, doubt and despair and God will give good gifts to us. When all other reasons for hope fail us, we can return to the God of hope because he is greater than our disappointment, greater than our failure, greater than the problems and conflicts in our hearts and our homes and our communities and our world. (Dale and Juanita Ryan, *Rooted in God's Love* [Downers Grove, Ill.: Inter-Varsity Press, 1992], pp. 241-42.)

Question 7. There are many reasons that it is a struggle to hope. Sometimes it seems that there is no reason to hope, that all evidence points to the contrary. Sometimes it seems like too much of a risk to hope, because we do not feel we can live through another disappointment.

Study 12. A Prayer of Joy. Psalm 66.

Purpose: To teach us how to express joy.

Question 5. The joy in this section is related to the experience of being delivered from danger. Encourage the group to discuss how the experience of coming through a difficult time can lead to joy.

Question 6. Giving materially puts many things into perspective. It is a tangible way of expressing the truth that all we have comes from God and belongs to God. It is a tangible way of saying thank you. And expressing gratitude is very closely related to expressing joy.

Question 8. Here joy is related to the experience of being personally loved. You might help the group discuss the relationship between experiencing God's love in personal ways and experiencing joy.

Question 12. Encourage the group to focus on the expression of joy as an act of intimate relating to God. This is one reason that joy is important. It is also important because we need to allow ourselves to experience the full rainbow of emotions God made us capable of feeling.

Juanita Ryan is a mental health nurse specialist with a private counseling practice in Brea, California. She and her husband, Dale, have authored sixteen Life Recovery Guides and Rooted in God's Love (IVP).